Short Walks in
Northumbria

Guide to 20 easy walks of 3 hours or less

Published by Collins
An imprint of HarperCollins Publishers
Westerhill Road
Bishopbriggs
Glasgow G64 2QT

www.harpercollins.co.uk

First edition 2011

Copyright © HarperCollins Publishers Ltd 2010

Original text © Richard Hallewell

Collins © is a registered trademark of
HarperCollins Publishers Limited

Mapping on the inner front cover and all
walking planning maps generated from
Collins Bartholomew digital databases

This product uses map data licensed from
Ordnance Survey ® with the permission of the
Controller of Her Majesty's Stationery Office.
© Crown copyright. Licence number 399302

Printed in China by South China Printing Co. Ltd.

ISBN 978 0 00 739540 8
Imp 002

email: roadcheck@harpercollins.co.uk

Contents

Introduction

Weardale

Walking in Northumbria

Northumbria, more than many other walking areas, is distinguished by the sheer diversity of its landscapes. Flat sandy beaches, dramatic sea cliffs, gentle rural vales, hilltop moorland, rocky peaks as well as an abundance of historic sites and wildlife provide the walker with a huge variety of walking possibilities. Excellent walks are found in the greatest concentration in the Pennine and Cheviot Hills and along the Northumbrian coast, but there are many fine footpaths and Rights of Way throughout the entire region.

In addition, there are a number of established long-distance footpaths in Northumbria. The longest of these is the Pennine Way, but shorter routes include the Cleveland Way (in the southeast of the area), the Weardale Way (from Monkwearmouth to Cowshill), the Derwent Walk Country Park (to the west of Newcastle), and the Waskerley Way, Brandon Bishop Auckland Walk, Lanchester Valley Walk and Deerness Valley Walk (a series of footpaths following the old railway lines to the west of Durham).

Visitors to the Cheviot and Pennine hills should bear in mind that navigation amongst the mass of similarly rounded peaks and buttresses can be tricky, even in clear conditions. There is one other hazard for hill walkers which is entirely predictable. From August onwards grouse shooting takes place on the moors so if you are planning to explore one of the hill routes, check with the local estate or tourist office before doing so.

Walking is a pastime which can fulfil the needs of everyone. You can adapt it to suit your own preferences and it is one of the healthiest of activities. This guide is for those who just want to walk a few miles. It really doesn't take long to find yourself in some lovely countryside. All the walks are five miles or less so should easily be completed in under three hours. Walking can be anything from an individual pastime to a family stroll, or maybe a group of friends enjoying the fresh air and open spaces of our countryside. There is no need for walking to be competitive and, to get the most from a walk, it shouldn't be regarded simply as a means of covering a given distance in the shortest possible time.

What is Northumbria?

Those with an interest in Anglo-Saxon history may consider the title of this book a little misleading. The ancient kingdom of Northumbria assumed many shapes and sizes during its 350 year existence (between AD 604, when it was created by Ethelfrid, and AD 954, when King Edred incorporated it into England), but its core is generally defined as lying between the Rivers Forth and Humber. The 'Northumbria' shown here, and used as the geographical basis for this book, is contained within the regional boundaries of Northumberland, Durham, Cleveland and Tyne and Wear - that is, the old (pre-1974) counties of Northumberland and Durham, plus a little of the North Riding of Yorkshire.

The word 'Northumbria' instantly conjures up a number of iconic images: Durham Cathedral, Geordie coal miners, Holy Island and the intricate tracery of the Lindisfarne Gospels, the bare slopes of the Cheviots, a gaunt peel tower and Hadrian's Wall. In a way, this list provides a key to the major historic periods in the area. The wall is evidence of the time of the Romans, who annexed all of this area at one time or another, while Holy Island reflects the Anglo-Saxon Northumbrians who followed them, and the island's priory and renowned illuminated manuscripts represent the Celtic people who predated both invasions, and who returned to the island bringing the Christian religion with them - only to be evicted by the Vikings. Durham Cathedral is also a symbol of Christianity - it is the burial place of St Cuthbert, the patron saint of Northumbria - but in addition demonstrates the power of the Prince Bishops: a virtually autonomous power in the north, they existed as a buffer between southern England and the Scots. The peel (or pele) tower characterises the three centuries of continuous warfare fought along the line of the Scottish Border, while the bare Cheviots portray the desolation in which these struggles occurred. And, lastly, the miner embodies the coal-mining industry, which underpinned the industrial strength of the North East during the 19th century.

Teesdale

Geology

The underlying geology of Northumbria is sedimentary of carboniferous age rocks with widespread intrusions of igneous rocks such as the Whin Sill. This rugged series of east–west ridges were exploited by the Romans who began building the 72 mile (117km) long Hadrian's Wall in AD 122. Another igneous outcrop is that of The Cheviots which were formed by volcanic action. At their heart is the granite mass of The Cheviot 2674ft (815m). This is surrounded by an area of old red sandstone, between the River Till and Redesdale; while the lower hills at the southern end of the range are composed of carboniferous limestone.

The Pennines are a low-rising mountain range often described as the 'backbone of England' and consist of a carboniferous limestone overlain with millstone grit. This limestone is exposed at the surface in the north of the chain but the general character of the range is that of moorland indented by more fertile river valleys. The Cleveland Hills are also topped by moorland but are formed by soft Lower Jurassic rocks interspersed with hard Middle Jurassic sandstone creating features such as the landmark peak of Roseberry Topping.

Wildlife in Northumbria

There is a wide variety of natural habitats in Northumbria, ranging from the damp moorland of the Cheviots and Pennines, through the sheltered dales and eastern farmland, to the raw North Sea coast, with its mud flats and sand dunes. Within this area are two large Nature Reserves - the mud flats and dunes of Lindisfarne and the open moorland of Upper Teesdale. The area is divided into a number of separate environments - Commercial Forestry, Woodland, Hills and Moorland, Farmland, Freshwater, and Seashore.

There was little coniferous woodland in Northumbria until commercial forestry began in the 1920s. A number of large forests are found throughout the area, and one positively huge one at Kielder, on the southern hills of the Cheviots. These plantations provide cover for rabbit, fox, red and grey squirrel and roe deer. The trees planted are quite varied and can include Scots and lodge-pole pine, Sitka and Norway spruce, Japanese and European larch, Douglas fir and others. Within these habitats it may be possible to spot crossbill, siskin, goldcrest, coal tit, redpoll and long-eared owl.

The original forest of broad-leaved trees which once covered much of Northumbria has now virtually disappeared, although small patches can be found along some of the routes in the book.

Woodland can provide the richest of inland habitats. Common species of trees throughout Northumbria include oak, hazel, beech, yew, ash, hawthorn and sycamore, with alder, sallow and willow in riverside woods. These provide a breeding ground for insects (the oak being particularly rich in this respect) which in turn attract birds such as pied and spotted flycatchers, green and great spotted woodpeckers, treecreeper, willow warbler and blackcap. Other woodland species include the wren, blackbird, song thrush, blue tit and great tit, plus birds of prey, such as the sparrowhawk and tawny owl.

Woodland mammals include small mice, voles and shrews, and the larger fox, badger, hedgehog, red and grey squirrel, roe deer, weasel and stoat. On the woodland floor, common wild flower species include foxglove, primrose, wood sorrel, lesser celandine, wood anemone, violet and bluebell.

The rounded hills of the Cheviots and the Pennines are covered in large swathes of grass and heather moorland. Each spring, areas of heather will be burnt from the moors to encourage new growth, which, in turn, attracts red grouse. This bird can be met on virtually any high-level walk, and is usually seen springing up from the heather with a loud, chuckling cry.

A rarer resident of the high ground is the peregrine falcon: a masterful flyer which takes its prey on the wing. Other birds of prey include the merlin and the hen harrier, while the short-eared owl can sometimes be seen hawking over the moors. Other birds to be found on the moors include the blackcock, snipe, curlew, lapwing, carrion crow and wheatear.

On heather moors the customary cover is ling heather, while damp areas of moor support bog cotton, bog asphodel, bog mosses and cranberry. In Upper Teesdale, however, the cover is sufficiently different to have warranted the establishment of a Nature Reserve where some plant species such as the spring gentian, Teesdale violet and alpine forget-me-not have been present since the end of the last Ice Age.

Farmland extends over a huge proportion of Northumbria. On the flat, coastal areas the land is almost entirely arable, while on the inland hills it is a mixture of arable and grazing. With all this variety, it is difficult to generalise about species. However, plants which may be found throughout the farmland include coltsfoot, dandelion, scabious, birdsfoot trefoil, cowslip, bugle and tufted vetch.

Many of the lower fields are lined with hedges, which encourage finches, sparrows, robin, linnet, wren, blackbird, thrushes and others, while larger birds include magpie, lapwing, curlew, snipe, pheasant and partridge plus redwing, fieldfare and waxwing in the winter months. Of birds of prey, the one most seen over farmland is the kestrel.

In Northumbria there is one semi-domesticated species worthy of note: the wild white cattle of Chillingham Castle (southeast of Wooler). This small herd is considered to be the purest remnant of the cattle of Bronze Age England.

The freshwater habitat is rather broad, covering everything from upland bogs to wide rivers and lakes. In the upper waters, the most common birds are the dipper and the grey and pied wagtails, which feed off insect larvae in the streams, as do tiny trout which can readily be seen in the larger pools. Often these waters will flow through narrow, wooded valleys. In such places, the kingfisher may be glimpsed, while more open water may attract heron, coot, moorhen, dabchick, great crested grebe and a variety of duck species. There are few mammals which specifically live by the water, but both the otter and the mink are present in this area.

Any naturalist reflecting on the Northumbrian coast brings to mind immediately the Fame Islands: a small archipelago offshore from Bamburgh. These small, rocky islands are incredibly rich in breeding seabirds - including puffin, guillemot, kittiwake, fulmar, razorbill, cormorant, shag and eider duck - while also having a colony of grey seals.

There is a small area of tidal mud at the mouth of the River Tees, and a larger one around Holy Island and Budle Bay, incorporated into what is now the Lindisfarne National Nature Reserve. The mud flats are of particular interest for the large numbers of wildfowl and waders. Wildfowl to be seen during the winter months include mallard, teal, wigeon and pintail, greylag and pale-bellied brent. While, of waders, there are greenshank, redshank, curlew, whimbrel, sanderling, little stint, bar-tailed godwit, dunlin, knot, oystercatcher and turnstone.

As well as mud flats, the Nature Reserve includes large areas of sand dunes, both on the island and on the mainland. These moving masses of loose sand are bound together by marram grass, while other plants to be found in this dry environment include hound's tongue, viper's bugloss and bloody cranesbill. Holy Island also has breeding colonies of little and sandwich terns.

Northumbria National Parks
Walkers can enjoy the scenic wilderness of two contrasting National Parks found in Northumbria. The Northumberland National Park was designated in 1956 and stretches from Hadrian's Wall in the south to the Cheviot Hills and Scottish border in the north covering a total of 405 square miles (1,049 sq km). From Iron Age hillforts to the legacy of the Romans and remnants of the Victorian industrial age, the sites of interest are numerous. Three informative National Park Centres are situated in Rothbury, Ingram and Once Brewed near Hadrian's Wall. 'The Wall' can be seen at many locations but 28 miles (46km) of the best preserved sections lie within the Northumberland National Park and include the World Heritage Site at Housesteads.

The northern edge of the North York Moors National Park is also featured in this book. Designated a National Park in 1952, this is one of the largest expanses of heather moorland in the United Kingdom and covers a total of 554 square miles (1,436 sq km). The spectacular scenery where the Cleveland Hills meet the North Sea has been declared Heritage Coast and the Boulby cliffs rising to 690ft (210m) are

Old alum quarries

the highest point on the east coast of England. This popular recreational expanse of countryside includes the Cleveland Way, a long distance walk encircling the moorland plateau with far reaching, wide-open views.

Walking tips & guidance

Safety

As with all other outdoor activities, walking is safe provided a few simple commonsense rules are followed:

- Make sure you are fit enough to complete the walk;

- Always try to let others know where you intend going, especially if you are walking alone;

- Be clothed adequately for the weather and always wear suitable footwear;

- Always allow plenty of time for the walk, especially if it is longer or harder than you have done before;

- Whatever the distance you plan to walk, always allow plenty of daylight hours unless you are absolutely certain of the route;

- If mist or bad weather come on unexpectedly, do not panic but instead try to remember the last certain feature which you have passed (road, farm, wood, etc.). Then work out your route from that point on the map but be sure of your route before continuing;

- Do not dislodge stones on the high edges: there may be climbers or other walkers on the lower crags and slopes;

- Unfortunately, accidents can happen even on the easiest of walks. If this should be the case and you need the help of others, make sure that the injured person is safe in a place where no further injury is likely to occur. For example, the injured person should not be left on a steep hillside or in danger from falling rocks. If you have a mobile phone and there is a signal, call for assistance. If, however, you are unable to contact help by mobile and you cannot leave anyone with the injured person, and even if they are conscious, try to leave a written note explaining their injuries and whatever you have done in the way of first aid treatment. Make sure you know exactly where you left them and then go to find assistance. Make your way to a telephone, dial 999 and ask for the police or mountain rescue. Unless the accident has happened within easy access of a road, it is the responsibility of the police to arrange evacuation. Always give accurate directions on how to find the casualty and, if possible, give an indication of the injuries involved;

- When walking in open country, learn to keep an eye on the immediate foreground while you admire the scenery or plan the route ahead. This may sound difficult but will enhance your walking experience;

- It's best to walk at a steady pace, always on the flat of the feet as this is less tiring. Try not to walk directly up or downhill. A zigzag route is a more comfortable way of negotiating a slope. Running directly downhill is a major cause of erosion on popular hillsides;

- When walking along a country road, walk on the right, facing the traffic. The exception to this rule is, when approaching a blind bend, the walker should cross over to the left and so have a clear view and also be seen in both directions;

- Finally, always park your car where it will not cause inconvenience to other road users or prevent a farmer from gaining access to his fields. Take any valuables with you or lock them out of sight in the car.

Equipment

Equipment, including clothing, footwear and rucksacks, is essentially a personal thing and depends on several factors, such as the type of activity planned, the time of year, and weather likely to be encountered.

All too often, a novice walker will spend money on a fashionable jacket but will skimp when it comes to buying footwear or a comfortable rucksack. Blistered and tired feet quickly remove all enjoyment from even the most exciting walk and a poorly balanced rucksack will soon feel as though you are carrying a ton of bricks. Well designed equipment is not only more comfortable but, being better made, it is longer lasting.

Clothing should be adequate for the day. In summer, remember to protect your head and neck, which are particularly vulnerable in a strong sun and use sun screen. Wear light woollen socks and lightweight boots or strong shoes. A spare pullover and waterproofs carried in the rucksack should, however, always be there in case you need them.

Winter wear is a much more serious affair. Remember that once the body starts to lose heat, it becomes much less efficient. Jeans are particularly unsuitable for winter wear and can sometimes even be downright dangerous.

Waterproof clothing is an area where it pays to buy the best you can afford. Make sure that the jacket is loose-fitting, windproof and has a generous hood. Waterproof overtrousers will not only offer complete protection in the rain but they are also windproof. Do not be misled by flimsy nylon 'showerproof' items. Remember, too, that garments made from rubberised or plastic material are heavy to carry and wear and they trap body condensation. Your rucksack should have wide, padded carrying straps for comfort.

It is important to wear boots that fit well or shoes with a good moulded sole – blisters can ruin any walk! Woollen socks are much more comfortable than any other fibre. Your clothes should be comfortable and not likely to catch on twigs and bushes.

It is important to carry a compass, preferably one of the 'Silva' type as well as this guide. A smaller scale map covering a wider area can add to the enjoyment of a walk. Binoculars are not essential but are very useful for spotting distant stiles and give added interest to viewpoints and wildlife. Although none of the walks in this guide venture too far from civilisation, on a hot day even the shortest of walks can lead to dehydration so a bottle of water is advisable.

Finally, a small first aid kit is an invaluable help in coping with cuts and other small injuries.

Public Rights of Way

In 1949, the National Parks and Access to the Countryside Act tidied up the law covering rights of way. Following public consultation, maps were drawn up by the Countryside Authorities of England and Wales to show all the rights of way. Copies of these maps are available for public inspection and are invaluable when trying to resolve doubts over little-used footpaths. Once on the map, the right of way is irrefutable.

Right of way means that anyone may walk freely on a defined footpath or ride a horse or pedal cycle along a public bridleway. No one may interfere with this right and the walker is within his rights if he removes any obstruction along the route, provided that he has not set out purposely with the intention of removing that obstruction. All obstructions should be reported to the local Highways Authority.

In England and Wales rights of way fall into three main categories:

- Public Footpaths – for walkers only;

- Bridleways – for passage on foot, horseback, or bicycle;

- Byways – for all the above and for motorized vehicles

Free access to footpaths and bridleways does mean that certain guidelines should be followed as a courtesy to those who live and work in the area. For example, you should only sit down to picnic where it does not interfere with other walkers or the landowner. All gates must be kept closed to prevent stock from straying and dogs must be kept under close control – usually this is interpreted as meaning that they should be kept on a leash. Motor vehicles must not be driven along a public footpath or bridleway without the landowner's consent.

A farmer can put a docile mature beef bull with a herd of cows or heifers, in a field crossed by a public footpath. Beef bulls such as Herefords (usually brown/red colour) are unlikely to be upset by passers by but dairy bulls, like the black and white Friesian, can be dangerous by nature. It is, therefore, illegal for a farmer to let a dairy bull roam loose in a field open to public access.

The Countryside and Rights of Way Act 2000 (the 'right to roam') allows access on foot to areas of legally defined 'open country' – mountain, moor, downland, heath and registered common land. You will find these areas shaded orange on the maps in this guide. It does not allow freedom to walk anywhere. It also increases protection for Sites of Special Scientific Interest, improves wildlife enforcement legislation and allows better management of Areas of Outstanding Natural Beauty.

Route marker

The Country Code

The Country Code has been designed not as a set of hard and fast rules, although they do have the backing of the law, but as a statement of commonsense. The code is a gentle reminder of how to behave in the countryside. Walkers should walk with the intention of leaving the place exactly as it was before they arrived. There is a saying that a good walker 'leaves only footprints and takes only photographs', which really sums up the code perfectly.

Never walk more than two abreast on a footpath as you will erode more ground by causing an unnatural widening of paths. Also try to avoid the spread of trodden ground around a boggy area. Mud soon cleans off boots but plant life is slow to grow back once it has been worn away.

Have respect for everything in the countryside, be it those beautiful flowers found along the way or a farmer's gate which is difficult to close.

Stone walls were built at a time when labour costs were a fraction of those today and the special skills required to build or repair them have almost disappeared. Never climb over or onto stone walls; always use stiles and gates.

Dogs which chase sheep can cause them to lose their lambs and a farmer is within his rights if he shoots a dog which he believes is worrying his stock.

The moors and woodlands are often tinder dry in summer, so take care not to start a fire. A fire caused by something as simple as a discarded cigarette can burn for weeks, once it gets deep down into the underlying peat.

When walking across fields or enclosed land, make sure that you read the map carefully and avoid trespassing. As a rule, the line of a footpath or right of way, even when it is not clearly defined on the ground, can usually be followed by lining up stiles or gates.

Obviously flowers and plants encountered on a walk should not be taken but left for others passing to enjoy. To use the excuse 'I have only taken a few' is futile. If everyone only took a few the countryside would be devastated. If young wild animals are encountered they should be left well alone. For instance, if a fawn or a deer calf is discovered lying still in the grass it would be wrong to assume that it has been abandoned. Mothers hide their offspring while they go away to graze and browse and return to them at feeding time. If the animals are touched it could mean that they will be abandoned as the human scent might deter the mother from returning to her offspring. Similarly with baby birds, who have not yet mastered flight; they may appear to have been abandoned but often are being watched by their parents who might be waiting for a walker to pass on before coming out to give flight lesson two!

What appear to be harmful snakes should not be killed because firstly the 'snake' could be a slow worm, which looks like a snake but is really a harmless legless lizard, and second, even if it were an adder (they are quite common) it will escape if given the opportunity. Adders are part of the pattern of nature and should not be persecuted. They rarely bite unless they are handled; a foolish act, which is not uncommon; or trodden on, which is rare, as the snakes are usually basking in full view and are very quick to escape.

Map reading

Some people find map reading so easy that they can open a map and immediately relate it to the area of countryside in which they are standing. To others, a map is as unintelligible as ancient Greek! A map is an accurate but flat picture of the three-dimensional features of the countryside. Features such as roads, streams, woodland and buildings are relatively easy to identify, either from their shape or position. Heights, on the other hand, can be difficult to interpret from the single dimension of a map. The Ordnance Survey 1:25,000 mapping used in this guide shows the contours at 5 metre intervals. Summits and spot heights are also shown.

The best way to estimate the angle of a slope, as shown on any map, is to remember that if the contour lines come close together then the slope is steep – the closer together the contours the steeper the slope.

Learn the symbols for features shown on the map and, when starting out on a walk, line up the map with one or more features, which are recognisable both from the map and on the ground. In this way, the map will be correctly positioned relative to the terrain. It should then only be necessary to look from the map towards the footpath or objective of your walk and then make for it! This process is also useful for determining your position at any time during the walk.

Let's take the skill of map reading one stage further: sometimes there are no easily recognisable features nearby: there may be the odd clump of trees and a building or two but none of them can be related exactly to the map. This is a frequent occurrence but there is a simple answer to the problem and this is where the use of a compass comes in. Simply place the map on the ground, or other flat surface, with the compass held gently above the map. Turn the map until the edge is parallel to the line of the compass needle, which should point to the top of the map. Lay the compass on the map and adjust the position of both, making sure that the compass needle still points to the top of the map and is parallel to the edge. By this method, the map is orientated in a north-south alignment. To find your position on the map, look out for prominent features and draw imaginary lines from them down on to the map. Your position is where these lines cross. This method of map reading takes a little practice before you can become proficient but it is worth the effort.

How to use this book

This book contains route maps and descriptions for 20 walks, with areas of interest indicated by symbols (see below). For each walk particular points of interest are denoted by a number both in the text and on the map (where the number appears in a circle). In the text the route instructions are prefixed by a capital letter. We recommend that you read the whole description, including the fact box at the start of each walk, before setting out.

Route instruction
denoted by a capital letter in the text

Point of interest
denoted by a number in the text

▬▬▬ main route   •••••• alternative route   ► direction of walk

Key to walk symbols
At the start of each walk there is a series of symbols that indicate particular areas of interest associated with the route.

🕊 Birdlife

🐾 Other wildlife

❀ Wild flowers

☀ Good views

🏰 Historical interest

🌳 Woodland

⛏ Geology

📖 Literature

SCALE 1:25,000

0   0.25   0.5   0.75   1 kilometre

0   ¼   ½ mile

Please note the scale for walk maps is 1:25,000 unless otherwise stated
North is always at the top of the page

Norham is a small village by the River Tweed, chiefly famous for its fine 12th century castle, built by the Bishop of Durham. Also of significance is the Ladykirk and Norham bridge, opened in 1864 to replace an earlier wooden structure connecting England to Scotland. Even before the wooden bridge, there was a great ford providing a place to cross the river. St Aidan crossed the border here on his way from Iona to Lindisfarne (see walk 2) in AD635 and for centuries after, it became one of the most important crossings on the Tweed. It was here that Edward I of England met the Scots nobility in 1292 to decide on the future king of Scotland.

Norham

View south from the bridge over the River Tweed

Route instructions

1 Norham Castle: now a stately ruin on a mound above the river at the eastern end of the village – was one of the major English strongholds along the Border, and witnessed a great deal of fighting during the centuries of Anglo-Scottish warfare.

A For this walk, park in the centre of Norham 8 miles (13km) southwest of Berwick on the A698/B6470, and walk down the track from the village green to the river.

B Once at the river turn left, along what starts as a wide, clear track. The border runs along the centre of the river at this point, so the steep bank on the far side of the water

is in Scotland. When the track ends, continue along a rough path. When there is minimum foliage, there are fine views looking back to the castle while, to the left the parish church is visible across the farmland.

C Continue along the riverbank until the bridge is reached. Either climb up the steps and cross the road, or else follow the path under the four-span bridge and then cut left, over a stile, to rejoin the correct path; running beside a fence to the right of a field above the river.

D Near the end of the field there is a stile over the fence to the right. Cross this and then continue to a gate

Plan your walk

Berwick-upon-Tweed
Coldstream
Alnwick
Newcastle upon Tyne
Hexham
Sunderland
Durham
Barnard Castle
Middlesbrough
Darlington

DISTANCE: 2 miles (3km)

TIME: 1 hour

START/END: NT899473 Norham village green

TERRAIN: Easy

MAPS:
OS Explorer 339;
OS Landranger 74

onto the road. Turn left to return to Norham. There are additional footpaths by the river: westwards (turn right at the road) to Twizel Bridge, and eastwards (from beyond the castle) to Horncliffe and beyond.

2 To visit St Cuthberts parish church turn left as you return to the village.

In 1320 the church was occupied and fortified by Robert the Bruce during a siege of the castle and it is likely that an earlier 9th century church once stood beneath the current site. Parts of the original Norman church remain, but considerable rebuilding was undertaken in the 17th and 19th centuries.

Norham

St Cuthberts Church

> 66 A wonderfully varied circuit on a tidal island steeped in history taking in a pretty village, a ruined priory, a wide harbour, a landmark castle, sand dunes and sweeping coastal scenery 99

Holy Island, or Lindisfarne, is a small, square island; little more than a mile (1.5km) square, with one long, sandy promontory, the Snook, reaching out westwards towards the mainland. It is only an island for around half of each day; the rest of the time it is joined to the mainland by a road across a mile (1.5km) long causeway over the wide sands and mud-flats which are now incorporated into the Lindisfarne National Nature Reserve. It is a place of unique beauty, and of enormous historical importance. Indeed, it holds a place in English religious history which parallels the importance of Iona in Scotland.

Holy Island

View of mainland and Chapel remains from Holy Island

Route instructions

Plan your walk

Berwick-upon-Tweed
Coldstream
Alnwick
Newcastle upon Tyne
Hexham
Sunderland
Durham
Barnard Castle
Middlesbrough
Darlington

DISTANCE: 3½ miles (5.5km)

TIME: 1¾ hours

START/END: NU127420 Holy Island main car park

It is essential to check the local tide tables (check at tourist information centres or www.northumberland life.org/holy-island/) before planning a trip to the island

TERRAIN: Easy

MAPS:
OS Explorer 340;
OS Landranger 75

A Walk out of the car park and turn right, then turn left at the first junction and right at the next, and walk on down the main street. Turn left at the end of the street and walk on, down the street, and along the lane beyond which passes the church and continues down to the shore.

B Turn left, along the shore, then climb up on to a low ridge along the southern edge of the island. From this point there are fine views in all directions. Continue along the ridge until it drops down towards the harbour.

1 From this ridge there are good views looking down on Lindisfarne Priory ruins

which was once one of the most important centres of early Christianity in Anglo-Saxon England and it still remains a site of pilgrimage today. There is a museum on the edge of the village detailing the history and development of the priory.

C Join the track which runs along the head of the little bay, past the row of upturned fishing boats which are now used as sheds. On the north edge of the bay, the track joins a road leading out towards the castle – now owned by the National Trust and open to the public.

2 The castle is perched on a rocky ridge and is a

landmark visible from many miles of the Northumbrian coastline. It was originally a Tudor fort which was then converted into a private house in 1903.

D Walk beyond the castle, past the old lime kilns, and join the track which curves to the left, inland from Castle Point, to shadow the eastern edge of the island. Follow this track past a small lake.

E There is a stile across the track near the end of the lake. A short distance beyond, there is a kissing gate. Proceed through this and then, after about 100yds (90m), cut left along a grassy track. Immediately there is a fork in this track: take the

Holy Island

right-hand route. Continue along this path, which runs along the edge of the sand dunes on the northern edge of the island.

▶ When the track reaches a junction, turn left through a gate and follow a straight track back into the village.

It was from Iona that the earliest Celtic missionaries came to the island. King Oswald of Northumbria, during a period of misfortune, spent a number of years in exile in Scotland, during which time he was converted to Christianity. When he had re-established himself at Bamburgh (see walk 3) (a short distance to the south, along the coast), he sent to Iona for a missionary. In 635 St Aidan arrived and established a mission on Holy Island, within sight of his patron's castle.

The mission was spectacularly successful, and remained a centre of religion and learning until, in June 793, the Vikings arrived. In this and subsequent raids the Christian centres in Northumberland were effectively destroyed. An attempt was made to rebuild the church on Holy Island, but by 875 the situation had become impossible and the island was deserted.

Following the period of Viking rule the island was reinhabited by a cell of Benedictine monks, at the end of the 11th century. It was they who built the priory – dedicated to the most famous Bishop of Lindisfarne, St Cuthbert. The building survived the ravages of the Border wars, before falling during the dissolution of the monasteries, in 1541, at which time much of the stone was removed for use in the construction of the castle – intended as a further defence against the Scots.

The Lough and dunes on Holy Island

> 66 A scenic coastal walk passing one of the largest inhabited castles in the country whilst enjoying far reaching views to the Farne Islands 99

As well as its great castle Bamburgh enjoys a varied coastline of sweeping beaches, dunes and rocky shores. A few miles north of Bamburgh is Budel Bay, a vast expanse of mud flats, home to thousands of sea and land birds. This bay was an important port in the 13th century but the harbour has long since disappeared beneath the sands and silt. The tidal sands now provide a home to wintering wildfowl and wading birds. Species such as greylag and pink-footed geese, mallard, and wigeon migrate here in late summer from the Arctic to spend the winter months in this southern corner of the Lindisfarne National Nature Reserve.

Bamburgh

Harkess Rocks

Route instructions

1 The impressive structure of Bamburgh Castle dominates this village: a great mass of red sandstone on an abrupt dolerite rock above the North Sea. The rock has been used as a stronghold from at least Anglo-Saxon times, but the oldest section of the building still in use is the great keep, dating from the 12th century. Additions and repairs to the structure were still being made at the turn of the century. The castle is open to the public for part of the year.

A Starting from the centre of Bamburgh, walk north on a street called 'The Wynding' to the edge of the village and then cut down to the sandy shore. If the tide

is in, it may be necessary to follow the road, and the path beyond, a little inland from the coast; but otherwise it is best to walk along the shore, across the sands and over the Harkess Rocks. Continue beyond, round the point to Budle Bay – a large tidal inlet of mud and sand, of particular interest for its sand dunes, and for the large numbers of wildfowl and waders which it attracts.

B Either return by the same route or skirt the caravan park to Kiln point. If the tide is out, bear right at the caravan park and walk this stretch along the beach before turning left up a track to the road. Otherwise follow the left

Plan your walk

DISTANCE: 5 miles (8km)

TIME: 2½ hours

START/END: NU180349 Bamburgh

TERRAIN: Easy

MAPS:
OS Explorer 340;
OS Landranger 75

Bamburgh

path above the caravan site and across fields to the road. The B1342 back to Bamburgh is a pleasant enough walk, but it can be busy during the summer, and should then be avoided.

2 Another attraction of Bamburgh is the charming Grace Darling Museum. The centrepiece of the collection is the coble (the traditional fishing boat of the North East) in which Grace and her father rescued the crew of the SS Forfarshire in 1838. Opposite the museum is St Aidan's Church containing a window depicting the heroics of Grace Darling and the churchyard is home to the ornate Grace Darling Memorial.

Grace Darling Memorial

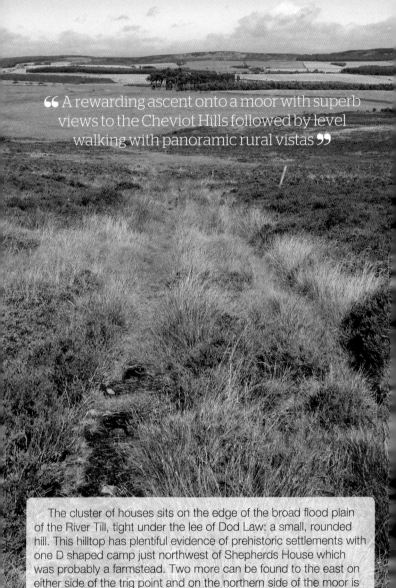

> **“** A rewarding ascent onto a moor with superb views to the Cheviot Hills followed by level walking with panoramic rural vistas **”**

The cluster of houses sits on the edge of the broad flood plain of the River Till, tight under the lee of Dod Law: a small, rounded hill. This hilltop has plentiful evidence of prehistoric settlements with one D shaped camp just northwest of Shepherds House which was probably a farmstead. Two more can be found to the east on either side of the trig point and on the northern side of the moor is a more extensive fort called The Ringses.

Views across Doddington Moor

Doddington

Shepherds House

Plan your walk

Berwick-upon-Tweed
Coldstream
Alnwick
Newcastle upon Tyne
Hexham
Sunderland
Durham
Barnard Castle
Middlesbrough
Darlington

DISTANCE: 3½ miles (5.5km)

TIME: 1¾ hours

START/END: NT999324 Doddington

TERRAIN: Moderate; one climb of 450ft (140m)

MAPS: OS Explorer 340; OS Landranger 75

Route instructions

A Park in the centre of the village and start walking up the road signposted to 'Wooler Golf Course'. In summer when the bracken covers the slopes, the hillside paths are impassable so continue up the lane and turn right to the golf course after which the track traverses Doddington Moor all the way to Shepherds House. In winter follow the lane but after 100yds (90m), turn hard right over a stile by a sign for 'Dodlaw'. The path beyond is not clear. Follow the fence to the right until a line of hawthorn trees appears up the slope to the left. Climb up to this line and follow it to a fence. Cross the stile and carry on to the last hawthorn, a short distance ahead. Cut left from the tree, up a clearer path, to the top of the slope; then turn right, below the low wall of an Iron Age fort. The views across the valley from this stretch are very pleasant.

B On the winter route, continue along the path to Shepherds House. Pass in front of the cottage and then turn left, up the side of the little field behind. When the field ends, ignore the clear track ahead and cut half right, up on to the golf course. On the summer route take a sharp left just before Shepherds House.

The route is a little difficult at this point. Cut right towards a low ridge. Climb this and walk past the golf tee beyond to a stile over a fence. Beyond is an area of heather moorland. Bear left along a clear track, towards a small stand of conifers, visible about ½ mile (1km) to the northeast.

Walk towards the left-hand side of the plantation until you reach a crossroad of paths near a fence intersection.

C Proceed through a gate and then bear left across the

Doddington

slope below the conifers and along a grassy path through another gateway. Continue north to another fence, beyond which lies another Iron Age fort called The Ringses.

❶ The Ringses is an ancient hillfort once made up of three ramparts amongst which cup-and-ring carvings can be found on several rock faces.

▶ As there is no direct access to The Ringses turn left dropping down along the edge of a wooded gully and up the opposite side.

Head for the right hand edge of the quarry on the horizon and once this is reached find a stile onto the quarry access track, turn right and then left onto the lane back down to Doddington.

❷ In Doddington village the Anglican church of St Mary and St Michael stands on the site of a 12th century house of worship. A small watch-tower was built in 1826 within the grounds of the churchyard, manned by a night guard, to protect the graves from being robbed.

View of southern slopes of Dod Law

> A moderate walk in a quiet hidden valley on the edge of the Cheviot Hills taking in grazed farmland, riverside woodland, and open meadows

The small market town of Wooler in Glendale is a popular centre for exploring the Cheviot Hills. It lies by a stream called the Wooler Water part of which is also known, as 'Happy Valley'. This walk starts at the confluence of the Harthope and Carey Burns which rise in the Cheviots and join to create Wooler Water. The Harthope Valley was formed by a geological fault and the remote Harthope Linn waterfall can be found by continuing past the start of the walk and up this picturesque, tranquil valley.

Happy Valley

Meadow beside Coldgate Water

Route instructions

A Walk on along the road, towards the bridge across the Carey Burn. Cross this and then turn hard left, beside a fence; then left again, over a stile; and then right, across a footbridge over the Harthope Burn. Climb the slope beyond and walk on, with an oak wood spreading down the valley slope to the right. Take care on this section as it can be quite muddy.

B When a fence comes in from the right, go round it and cut right, on a well-trodden path. Continue in this direction until a dyke and a line of hawthorns cross ahead. Continue straight on and keep right of a large pond heading for a stile up the slope. Then cross a small footbridge and over the protected barbed wire after which the path is indistinct so bear left across the slope aiming for the top edge of a wood. If you are lucky you may see a brown hare leaping through the bracken on this hillside.

C Follow a clear path along the wood edge, through a protected area and onto a good track to reach North Middleton.

D Once the track reaches the road turn left, as far as the ford over the burn. To the left of the ford is a footbridge. Cross this and turn left, along a clear track through dense conifer and broad-leaved woodland by the burn side.

Plan your walk

- Berwick-upon-Tweed
- Coldstream
- Alnwick
- Newcastle upon Tyne
- Hexham
- Sunderland
- Durham
- Barnard Castle
- Middlesbrough
- Darlington

DISTANCE: 4 miles (6.5km)

TIME: 2 hours

START/END: NT976249 South of Wooler on the minor road to Langleeford, park in a grassy area to the right, just north of the Carey Burn

TERRAIN: Moderate; muddy sections

MAPS: OS Explorer OL 16; OS Landranger 75

Happy Valley

When the woodland ends continue across the grazing land on the flood plain, back to the bridge. Some sections are well used by cattle and can be very muddy. At one point the burn swings to the north, and it is necessary to follow a path through the gorse scrub up to the right.

Footbridge over Coldgate Water

66 Encompassing a pretty coastal village, a muddy estuary, riverside farmland and a fine sandy beach this a lovely varied walk **99**

Alnmouth is a fine sea-side village on a peninsula between the tidal mud of the Aln Estuary and the sands of Alnmouth Bay. In mediaeval times it was an important port, but now it is simply an unspoilt haven for small boats.

Alnmouth village at low tide

Alnmouth

Lesbury church

Route instructions

A Walk down to the southern end of the village and turn right along Riverside Road. Continue on this road until, just beyond a children's playground, a path (signed 'Lovers Walk') cuts to the left along the mud-flats.

B Follow this to the Duchess's Bridge, then climb up onto the bridge and turn left. Walk on a gravel path running beside the road for about ¼ mile (0.5km) until, a short distance before the school, a small gate opens into a playing field to the right.

C Follow the right hand edge of this playing field following a line of telegraph poles and then continue on a path parallel to a row of houses which starts to the left. Opposite the end of the row there is gate, after which the path cuts half left, leading across a field to another gate. This leads to a road, and then to a bridge over the Aln.

D Cross the bridge and bear right across the riverside grass to the fields. Alternatively, for a quick diversion into Lesbury village follow the track straight on from the bridge and turn right along the road. When the B1339 cuts left, turn right down a lane opposite running between the houses to the riverside grassy area where a left turn leads to the fields.

Plan your walk

DISTANCE: 4 miles (6.5km)

TIME: 2 hours

START/END: NU246103 Alnmouth

TERRAIN: Easy

MAPS:
OS Explorer 332;
OS Landranger 81

Berwick-upon-Tweed

Coldstream

Alnwick

Newcastle upon Tyne

Hexham

Sunderland

Durham

Barnard Castle

Middlesbrough

Darlington

E Follow the path through three fields gradually veering away from the river before climbing the steep slope on the left to end up slightly to the right of a line of telegraph poles. Once at the top of the slope, cross a stile, and the road beyond, and walk down the driveway into Alnmouth Golf Club, directly opposite.

F Follow the drive down to the club house. When a wall starts on the left-hand side, walk down a path to the left of it, leading down to a fine sandy shore, and then turn right to return to Alnmouth. If the sea is rough use an alternative route by turning right immediately in front of the clubhouse and follow the cliff path back to Alnmouth passing between two golf greens on the way.

Alnmouth

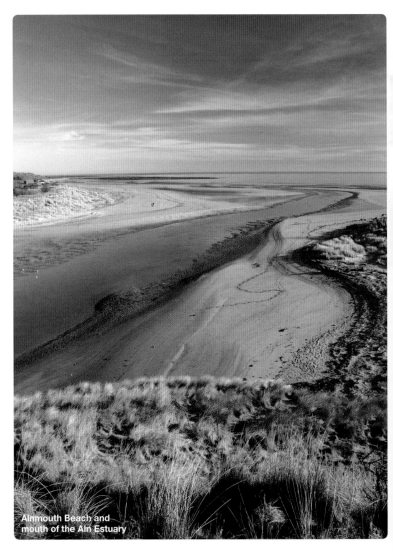

Alnmouth Beach and
mouth of the Aln Estuary

> **A circumnavigation of beautiful, open moorland providing exhilarating, panoramic views in many directions**

Rothbury is a pleasant country town, climbing up the steep slopes on either side of a narrow stretch of Coquetdale. The first mention of Rothbury was around the year 1100 and it was chartered as a market town in 1291 becoming an important centre for dealing in cattle and wool. Surrounded by stunning countryside in the shape of moorland, crags, dales and woodland it has become a welcoming centre for many outdoor activities and affords abundant scenic walking opportunities.

Track across moorland
north of Rothbury

Rothbury

Moorland cairn with views of Rothbury

Route instructions

Berwick-upon-Tweed

Coldstream

Alnwick

Newcastle upon Tyne

Hexham

Sunderland

Durham

Middlesbrough

Barnard Castle

Darlington

DISTANCE: 5 miles (6.5km)

TIME: 2½ hours

START/END: NU057017 Rothbury

TERRAIN: Moderate; one 500ft (150m) climb

MAPS:
OS Explorer 332;
OS Landranger 81

A Start walking from the centre of the town. Walk up Providence Lane (leading north from the eastern end of the High Street), then continue steeply up the hill to join Hillside Road, on the northern edge of the town. On the far side of the road, a sign indicates a footpath to Cartington. Continue in the direction of this sign up Blaeberry Hill and as the road bends left continue straight ahead on a path between two fences. Then follow a rough path past the left hand edge of a wood and on to the moor. Climb directly up the slope ahead to join a track running across the hill towards the plantation. Turn right along a clear track, taking note of this junction for the return to

Rothbury at the end of the moorland circuit.

B As it approaches the trees, a yellow arrow indicates the start of a clear path leading off to the left. Follow this path across an area of open moorland towards another plantation.

C Cross a stile into this plantation and turn right along a grassy track. At a T-junction in the wood, cut right signed 'Alnwick Road (B6341)', down to Primrose Cottage on the edge of the trees.

D From the cottage, turn left on a clear track running along the edge of the plantation, signposted to 'Thropton and Rothbury'.

Continue along this track. At one point it is crossed by another track: carry straight on through a gate and then through woodland.

E At the far end of the wood the track emerges once more onto the moor. Initially it heads westwards, towards another plantation, but then it cuts to the south, winding across the moorland and providing fine views of Coquetdale and the Simonside Hills (see walk 8). Continue on this track until it rejoins the path from Rothbury, then turn right to return to the start.

Rothbury

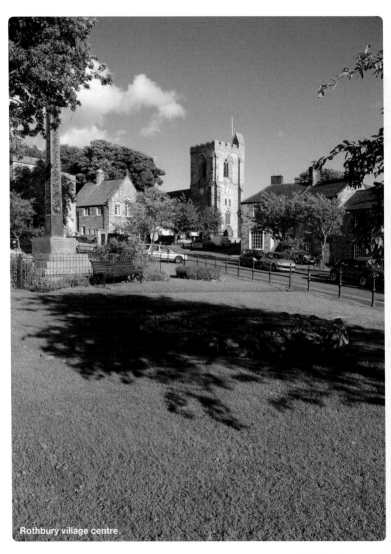

Rothbury village centre

Rothbury is a fine old country town, in a narrow section of Coquetdale, pressed between a steep slope to the north (see walk 7) and the forestry covered slopes and ridges of the Simonside Hills to the south.

Simonside

Views of Rothbury from Simonside Ridge

Route instructions

1 There are three routes through the forest, the two longest of which – the Ravens Heugh Walk and the Simonside Ridge Walk – lead up to the pronounced rocky ridges which rise up above the forest to the south. These ridges are of sandstone, and are similar in composition and form to those in Thrunton Forest to the north.

A For the Ravens Heugh walk follow the well-marked orange arrows and for the Simonside Ridge Walk follow the red arrows. Both follow winding tracks up through the conifers. The shorter Ravens Heugh path has only a brief section on the open hillside but, as the name suggests, the

Simonside Ridge path, follows a stone slab path up and along a line of crags from which there are fine views of Rothbury and Thropton, and of the hills to the north of Coquetdale.

B There is one possible alteration to the paths indicated. The Simonside Ridge route climbs on to the ridge of heather and stone and follows it eastwards to Dove Crag. From this point, instead of following the forest walk back into the trees, continue along the ridge on the path to the Beacon Cairn, and from there drop down to the quiet road below. Turn left along the road to return to the start of the walk.

Plan your walk

Berwick-upon-Tweed
Coldstream
Alnwick
Newcastle upon Tyne
Hexham
Sunderland
Durham
Barnard Castle
Middlesbrough
Darlington

DISTANCE: Up to 4½ miles (7.25km)

TIME: Up to 2¼ hours

START/END: NZ037997 Simonside car park off the minor road south east of Great Tosson village

TERRAIN: Moderate; one climb of 750ft (230m)

MAPS: OS Explorer OL 42; OS Landranger 81

Simonside

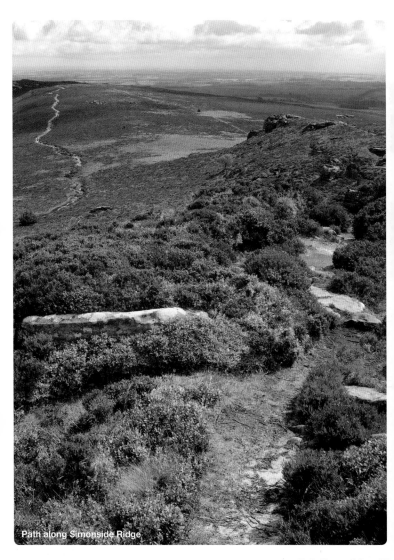

Path along Simonside Ridge

> *A linear path up a deep, wooded glen, crisscrossing a bubbling burn towards a dramatic waterfall*

The small town of Bellingham is the main centre for a large area around the valley of the River North Tyne (on which it sits), Redesdale and the massive Kielder Forest.

The Hareshaw Burn meets the River North Tyne in Bellingham and not far upstream is the delightful Hareshaw Linn waterfall. This Site of Special Scientific Interest is home to rare ferns and lichen as well as red squirrel, great spotted woodpecker and Daubenton's bat.

Woodland path approaching Hareshaw Linn

Hareshaw Linn

Footbridge over
Hareshaw Burn

Route instructions

Berwick-upon-Tweed
Coldstream
Alnwick
Newcastle
upon Tyne
Hexham
Sunderland
Durham
Barnard
Castle
Middlesbrough
Darlington

DISTANCE: 3 miles
(5km) there and back

TIME: 1½ hours

START/END: NY840834
Bellingham

TERRAIN: Easy

MAPS:
OS Explorer OL 42;
OS Landranger 80

A From the centre of
the town, turn down
the road signposted for
'Redesmouth'. The road
crosses the Hareshaw Burn
almost immediately. Cut
left directly after the bridge
on a road leading up to a
car park on the edge of the
town. From the car park, a
signpost indicates the start
of the footpath. The route
is quite clear. It starts by
climbing through an area of
open ground – the mounds
under the grass are the
remains of the 19th century
coal and iron-mining
industry – before entering
the mixed woodland around
the upper valley.

B In the woods the path
alternates between running
low down right beside the

burn and higher sections
giving views through the
trees. After a while the
path also winds back and
forth across the burn on a
sequence of footbridges
before finally entering a
rocky canyon at the head
of the valley. The highlight
of this glen is a fine
waterfall called Hareshaw
Linn of some 30ft (48m)
dropping through the gap
between two great blocks
of stone. At the end of the
path a small cave is cut into
the rocky wall to the right,
providing a dry viewing
point of this dramatic scene.

C Return by the same
route.

1 The most interesting
building in the town is

St Cuthbert's Church.
The earliest sections date
from the 13th century, but
later additions were made
in the early 17th and the
19th centuries. The place
is very strongly built, with
a heavy stone roof and slit
windows. The cannon balls
found in the roof during its
reconstruction are evidence
that, this close to the
Border, a building had to
be strong to survive.

Hareshaw Linn

Hareshaw Linn

> **A steeply undulating path running beside sections of Hadrian's Wall with magnificent views either side of this historic ridge**

When Hadrian's Wall was completed, in AD163, it stretched 73 miles (117km), from the Solway Firth in the west to the Tyne estuary in the east. For most of the following two centuries, it was to be the northern boundary of the Roman Empire in Britain.

The builders' search for the most easily defended route for their wall led them across the bleak land to the north of the River South Tyne, where they were able to utilise the outcrops of the Whin Sill, a recurring geological feature in Northumbria which produces a series of steep crags. Thus, the wall is not only a relic of great archeological interest, it is also scenically fascinating.

Hadrian's Wall looking east to Housesteads Crags

Hadrian's Wall

Hadrian's Wall from field near King's Wicket

Route instructions

A This route starts from the car park on the brow of the ridge at Steel Rigg just north of Once Brewed on the B6318. Walk east from the car park. The path starts on the top of the wall, then drops down and continues beside it; along the crags of Steel Rigg and through the woods above Crag Lough.

B At the far end of the lough, the path crosses the track leading back to Hotbank Farm. At this point it is possible to double back to the car park, by turning right down the track for a short distance, and then right again at the sign for a footpath, along the Roman road. This makes a walk of around 3 miles (5km). Otherwise, continue (leaving Hotbank beyond a dyke to the left) along the wall for a further mile (1.5km) to the great ruined fort at Housesteads (fee on entry).

1 Housesteads is the most well known fort on Hadrian's Wall and known to the Romans as 'Vercovicium', 'the place of effective fighters'. Added to the wall around AD124 the site covers an area of about 5 acres (2ha) and it was garrisoned by approximately 1,000 infantry. The overall fort the layout changed very little during its 3 centuries of occupation but the internal buildings went through various stages of modification evident in the remains exposed today.

Plan your walk

DISTANCE: 3–7½ miles (5–12km)

TIME: Up to 4 hours

START/END: NY750676 Steel Rigg car park

TERRAIN: Moderate/ Strenuous; with steep undulations

MAPS: OS Explorer OL 43; OS Landranger 86

Hadrian's Wall

C Continue along the right-hand side of the wall for a further ½ mile (1km) beyond Housesteads, dropping down from the steep summit of King's Hill until a stile appears to the left beside a gate named 'King's Wicket'. Looking westwards from the stile, the wall runs along a series of crags to the left, there is a marshy hollow beneath the crags, and, to the right, a ridge runs parallel to the wall.

D Turn left over the stile and follow the indistinct route over the marshy ground towards a small copse. Continue through the trees where the path can be muddy and head towards the Pennine Way enjoying fine views of the parallel ridge of crags to the left. At the intersection with the Pennine Way, turn left and climb uphill to return to the wall.

E Return to Steel Rigg along the original route to the right. When approaching Crag Lough there is the option to return by an alternative route as described in **B**.

Hadrian's Wall looking east to Crag Lough

> **A circuit through exhilarating moorland and hill-farmland around an old lead-mining settlement**

Allenheads sits at the very head of beautiful East Allen Dale; 1300ft (400m) above sea level. It is a tiny village, originally built to house people working in the lead mines of the area. There is a Heritage Centre in the village explaining its history, while the surrounding moorland is littered with the surviving traces of the industry.

Ruin on hillside above East Allen Dale

Allenheads

Curricks on moor above Allenheads

Route instructions

A Start from the centre of the village and head off up Rookhope Road. Follow this road as it climbs steeply for about ¾ mile (1.2km). A short distance after a cattle grid a clear track cuts off the road to the left. This leads past a quarry which once provided stone roof slates (an attractive feature of many of the buildings along this walk) up to the stone curricks on Dodd End.

B Follow the track right from the curricks, and continue with a dyke to the left after which the track traverses the side of the hill behind a string of fine ruins. There are views to the old mine workings across the dale.

C Pass behind Byerhope Farm then continue in the same direction until another track appears ahead. Turn right at this junction marked by a cairn and follow this track for a short distance up onto a ridge.

D Look out for a post with arrows marking the start of the bridleway on the left, back down to the road. Follow these posts which mark the descent and then cross the road at the bottom and walk down the minor road opposite as it zigzags down to the river.

E Cross the river and follow the road to the left. When it breaks to the right, continue along the riverside footpath. This eventually

Plan your walk

Berwick-upon-Tweed
Coldstream
Alnwick
Newcastle upon Tyne
Hexham
Sunderland
Durham
Barnard Castle
Middlesbrough
Darlington

DISTANCE: 5 miles (8km)

TIME: 2½ hours

START/END: NY859453 Allenheads

TERRAIN: Moderate; one climb of 600ft (180m)

MAPS:
OS Explorer OL 31;
OS Landranger 87

joins the road once again. Cut left, across the river, then right, to return to Allenheads.

1 In the village centre is a Heritage Centre depicting the lead-mining past of the village. This houses the important Armstrong water engine and a restored blacksmith's shop as well as a welcome café.

Allenheads

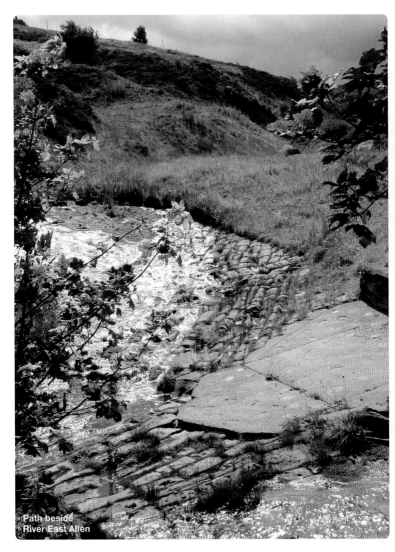

Path beside
River East Allen

> **This loop has a wonderful mixture of scenery from an enchanting village, to a peaceful valley, sweeping moorland and a delightful leafy riverside**

The village of Blanchland, though only small, is one of the finest in Northumbria, and its pastoral elegance comes as something of a surprise amidst the bleak moors and hills of the area. The greater part of the settlement was built in the 18th century, on the site of a 12th century abbey; but the great gate-house on one side of the square is older: it dates from the 15th century.

Ruin of an old lead mine in Shildon

Blanchland

Blanchland gate-house and post office

Plan your walk

Berwick-upon-Tweed

Coldstream

Alnwick

Newcastle upon Tyne

Hexham

Sunderland

Durham

Barnard Castle

Middlesbrough

Darlington

DISTANCE: 3½ miles (5.5km)

TIME: 1¾ hours

START/END: NY964504 Blanchland

TERRAIN: Moderate; gradual climb of 350ft (110m)

MAPS:
OS Explorer 307;
OS Landranger 87

Route instructions

A Park in the car park on the northern edge of the village and start walking up the metalled road beside the Shildon Burn; through woodland at first, but later through open farmland. As the farmland turns to moorland, the views across the Derwent Vale become more spectacular.

1 At one point, opposite Shildon, there is the ruin of an old lead mine on private land on the left-hand side of the road. The village of Blanchland was originally built to house lead miners.

B Follow the road up to Pennypie. When a track cuts right, up to the house, carry straight on through a gate in the wall. Then turn left at a path signed 'Baybridge', across a footbridge over the burn and on along a clear track through heather moorland. Watch for red grouse and curlew along this stretch.

C Follow the track until it joins a metalled road, then cut left down to the road. Looking across the valley, it is possible to see the chimneys of the old lead mines on the moors over towards Weardale.

D Turn right along the road until, just before it crosses the River Derwent, a footpath cuts off to the left, signposted for 'Blanchland'. Follow the uneven path along the riverside, through a narrow band of mixed woodland, back to the village.

2 Blanchland lies in the Upper Derwent Valley in the North Pennines Area of Outstanding Natural Beauty. This historic collection of buildings form the centrepiece of an estate owned by a charitable trust. The unspoilt qualities of this conservation village make it a frequent setting for 18th-century period films.

Blanchland

Signpost on Birkside Fell

> **"Rough paths and clear tracks leading through fine mixed woodland "**

A historic market town on the banks of the River Tyne, Hexham has many sites of interest. Its railway station is one of the oldest in the world, operational since 1835 and the oldest 'Gaol' in the country now tells the story of Hexham's past. The dominating building, however, is the 13th century Hexham Abbey built on the site of an earlier church and monastery dating back to AD 674. The Battle of Haxham in 1464 was regarded to be one of the decisive events in the War of the Roses but the exact location of this skirmish is in question. The popular view is that it took place on the Hexham Levels but an alternative suggestion is that Swallowship Wood was the more likely site being strategically placed on the crest of Swallowship Hill along the southern edge of this walk.

View looking north from path to Hexham

Hexham

Clearing in Halfmile Wood

Route instructions

A Park to the west of the road, near the entrance to Dukeshouse Wood Centre. Walk back down the road for about 400yds (0.3km). Turn right down the road signposted for Fellside.

B Turn right off the road at the signpost for the footpath to Duke's House, into an area of mixed woodland. There are a number of paths through the wood, and it is important to stick to the main one. This leads up a slope, bearing left along a felled, flatter section, then cutting hard right and running straight up (with a field to the left) to a junction with another track.

C Walk straight across the track and through a gap in

the fence opposite, then bear slightly left along a well-trodden path. After a short distance, another track cuts across ahead; walk straight across this and continue beyond. The path splits when it reaches a fence – walk left, along the line of the fence, and follow it down to the corner of a field; then cut left, then right, into a wood of pine trees.

D The path soon splits once more. Take the right-hand path through the wood and when a gully appears ahead, keep above and to the left of it, on a path which leads through an oak wood above the river.

E This path shortly crosses another, smaller gully. Bear

DISTANCE: 3½ miles (5.5km)

TIME: 1¾ hours

START/END: NY944630 B6306 on the southeast edge of Hexham

TERRAIN: Easy; 250ft (80m) undulating

MAPS:
OS Explorer OL 43;
OS Landranger 87

slightly to the left across this, through a gap in a crumbling dyke, and continue on the track beyond. A track soon cuts off to the left. Ignore this and carry straight on.

F Continue until a T-junction is reached,

then cut left and follow a clear track up hill to a further, four way junction.

G Turn left and follow a clear path which then becomes a track past the Duke's House and back to the B6306.

Hexham

1 Dukes House or 'the house of a thousand chimneys' is one of the largest neo-gothic country homes in Hexham. It's surrounded by a huge garden in the midst of extensive woodland and it was allegedly built on the site of a cottage where Henry Beaufort, 3rd Duke of Somerset, was captured in 1464 before being taken to Hexham and executed.

Rooftop of Duke's House

66 An easy, flat circuit starting along a pleasant, leafy track and returning along a delightful riverbank 99

The little town of Wylam holds an unrivalled position in the history of the railways. The line between Wylam Colliery and the port of Lemington – 5 miles (8km) down the Tyne carried the early steam locomotive Puffing Billy, built in 1813 by the pioneer William Hedley; while, by coincidence, the greatest name in the early history of rail, George Stephenson – the designer of The Rocket – was born in a little cottage by the side of the line. This path follows the route of the old line, and passes Stephenson's birthplace.

Wylam

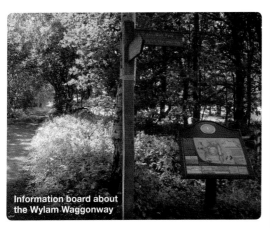

Information board about the Wylam Waggonway

Route instructions

A Park in the car park (once Wylam Station) close to the river. The path used for this route is part of a longer walkway, running from Newburn – 3 miles (5km) to the east – to Ovingham – 3 miles (5km) up river to the west.

For this walk, set off along the track signposted 'Wylam Waggonway' and 'Blayney Row'.

B After ½ mile (1km), look out for an information board on the left detailing the history of the Wyalm Waggonway. After this the track passes Stephenson's Cottage, which is now owned by the National Trust and is open to the public for restricted periods (check

with tourist offices for details). The track then continues between a golf course to the left and the tree-lined river to the right. Gradually, the track pulls away from the riverside, and, after a mile (1.5km), reaches a row of cottages.

1 Stephenson's Cottage was built around 1760 to accommodate mining families. George Stephenson was born here in 1781, where his whole family lived in the one room. After making his name at nearby Wylam colliery he went on to become an engineer and inventor who built the first public railway in the world to use steam locomotives. The cottage furnishings reflect the period of this

Plan your walk

Berwick-upon-Tweed
Coldstream
Alnwick
Newcastle upon Tyne
Hexham
Sunderland
Durham
Barnard Castle
Middlesbrough
Darlington

DISTANCE: 4½ miles (7km)

TIME: 2¼ hours

START/END: NZ118646 Wylam

TERRAIN: Easy

MAPS:
OS Explorer 316;
OS Landranger 88

Wylam

great rail pioneer, often referred to as the 'Father of Railways'.

▶ A mile (1.5km) further on down the track is the town of Newburn but, for this route, turn right at the cottages. This track leads in front of another terrace down to the river. Turn right along a paved path which soon becomes rough following the side of the Tyne – tidal as far up river as Wylam – to rejoin the original track.

Stephenson's Cottage

> "Three signposted forest walks on good tracks through beautiful mixed woodland within which are a variety of natural and industrial heritage sites"

Chopwell Wood is a fine, mixed forestry wood on the northern slopes above the River Derwent. The existence of the wood is recorded as early as the 12th century, when it was a part of the estates belonging to the Bishops of Durham. It is now in the ownership of the Forestry Commission but is a somewhat more interesting place than many other commercial woods, having a large number of broad-leaved trees interspersed amongst the conifers. This allows more air and light into the forest and encourages the undergrowth.

Sculpture on River Walk

Chopwell Wood

Old Railway Footpath

Route instructions

Plan your walk

Berwick-upon-Tweed

Coldstream

Alnwick

Hexham

Newcastle upon Tyne

Sunderland

Durham

Barnard Castle

Middlesbrough

Darlington

A On the B6315 at Hooker Gate, turn down a minor road leading to a car park in the forest from which there are three differently coloured, signposted walks. The two longer routes lead to a point giving views of the River Derwent through the trees and the River Walk continues along the top of the valley for a while, passing above a fine oak wood covering the slope down to the river. The trees in this part of the wood were planted after the Napoleonic Wars of the early 19th century, to replace those which had been taken to build ships for the English fleet.

1 For the Old Railway Footpath (1½ miles (2.4km)) follow the signposted blue

route along which can be found two restored coal wagons which once ran along the Chopwell & Garesfield Railway between 1896 and 1961 connecting the Chopwell Colliery to High Spen and from there on to the River Tyne.

2 For the River Walk (3½ miles (5.5km)) follow the red route along which is a sculpted bench commemorating the mining industry. Further along the path there are some 200 year old settling tanks that provided clean water for the Lintzford Paper Mill between 1785 and 1923. This was just one of several paper mills in the Derwent Valley operational during the 17th and 18th centuries.

DISTANCE: 1½ – 4½ miles (1–5km)

TIME: ¾ – 2¼ hours

START/END: NZ137584 Chopwell Wood car park off the B6315 at Hooker Gate

TERRAIN: Easy / Moderate; undulating

MAPS: OS Explorer 307; OS Landranger 88

3 For the Boundary Walk (4½ miles (7.25km)) follow the signposted green route which has various points of interest including the site of the Chopwell Colliery fan which was used to exchange bad air for good air in the mine. The path also passes 'The Bomb Ponds' which were created in World War II but are now a conservation site. The other pond passed near the golf course was created in the early 20th century as a source of water for fighting forest fires.

Chopwell Wood

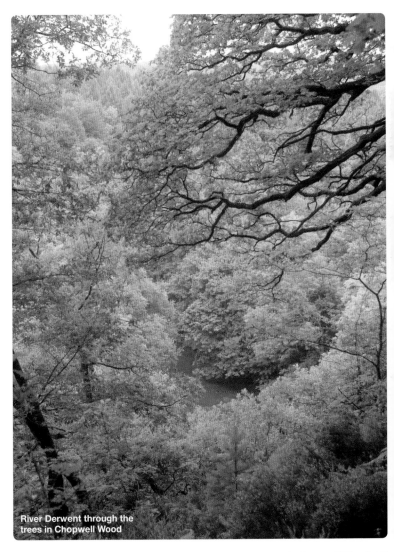

River Derwent through the trees in Chopwell Wood

66 Good pathways through a mixed farming and industrial landscape with a section on the Lanchester Valley Way **99**

On the western outskirts of the cathedral city of Durham is Neville's Cross; the site of a battle in 1346 between David II of Scotland and an army of northern English lords. The English were victorious, and the Scottish king was imprisoned in London for 11 years.

River Browney north of Bearpark

Bearpark

Views to Bearpark

Route instructions

A Park in Neville's Cross in a residential road off the busy A167 and start walking down Quarry House Lane – just to the north of the railway line. Follow this road until the sign indicates 'farm road only'; then cut left down a footpath along a wooded slope.

B After a short distance, there is a stile beside a gate leading into a field. Go over this and walk along the right-hand side of the field. When the field ends the path recommences, running along the side of the River Browney. When a bridge over the river is reached, turn left across it and follow the road beyond up to a farm.

C A short distance after the farm, the track is crossed by a disused railway line. Turn right along this former section of line (between Durham and Lanchester) now designated the 'Lanchester Valley Way'.

D After ¾ mile (1km) proceed across a farm track and then over a minor road beyond it. Continue along the track, under the shadow of a hill on which are perched the terraces of the mining village of Bearpark.

E After a further ¾ mile (1km), the track is crossed by another track. The Lanchester Valley path continues straight ahead, but for this route, cut right; down across the River Browney, past the slight ruins of the old Bishops'

Plan your walk

Berwick-upon-Tweed

Coldstream

Alnwick

Newcastle upon Tyne

Hexham

Sunderland

Durham

Barnard Castle

Middlesbrough

Darlington

DISTANCE: 4½ miles (7km)

TIME: 2¼ hours

START/END: NZ260422 Neville's Cross

TERRAIN: Moderate

MAPS:
OS Explorer 308;
OS Landranger 88

residence of Beau Repaire on a mound by the river, and up the short slope.

F A good track leads past two farms with great views across the River Browney Valley to Bearpark (a corruption of 'Beau Repaire') before gradually dropping down to the road. Turn left along the road (Tollhouse Road), which soon runs into housing as it returns to Neville's Cross.

Bearpark

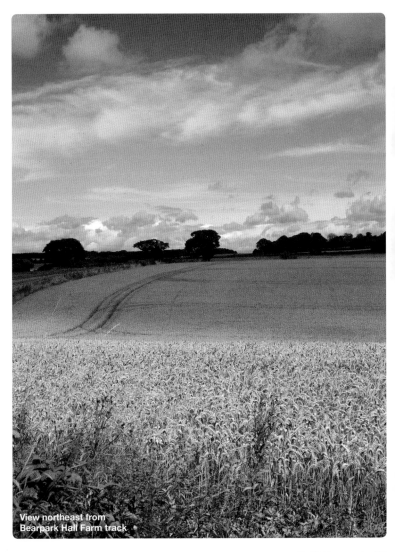

View northeast from
Bearpark Hall Farm track

> **A gentle path through attractive riverside woodland returning on a higher ridge beside pleasant open farmland**

This route enjoys a small section of the Teesdale Way which is a long distance path (100 miles (160km)) running between the North Sea and the Pennines. The town of Barnard Castle is the attractive, historic 'capital' of Teesdale and draws many visitors but only a few minutes walking leads to a tranquil path beside the River Tees.

River Tees from a footbridge

Barnard Castle

Ruins of Barnard Castle

Route instructions

A Walk down the right-hand side of the church in the centre of town. Behind this building there is a grassy space, on the far side of which are the ruins of 12th century Barnard Castle (fee on entry). Near the end of the church is a signpost indicating the direction for a number of local walks. For this route (shown on the signpost as 'Walk 1'), cut right along a tarmac road which gradually drops down to the bank of the River Tees.

B After a short distance a bridge cuts left, across the river. Ignore this and take the path which crosses the footbridge over the little Percy Beck and then continues by the riverside.

C Follow this path through mixed woodland, past the twin supports of a dismantled rail bridge, and then on, for a further mile (1.5km) or so, through a pleasant rocky gorge to a small meadow by the riverside. Watch out for deer in the quiet wooded glen areas.

D Go through a gate into this meadow and follow the dyke to the right for about 100yds (90m). When a gate appears to the right, go through it, then climb the wooded slope beyond to a fence by a field.

E Cross the fence and turn right. Continue through a succession of fields, keeping the woodland across the

Plan your walk

Berwick-upon-Tweed
Coldstream
Alnwick
Hexham
Newcastle upon Tyne
Sunderland
Durham
Barnard Castle
Middlesbrough
Darlington

DISTANCE: 4 miles (6.5km)

TIME: 2 hours

START/END: NZ049166 Barnard Castle

TERRAIN: Moderate

MAPS:
OS Explorer OL 31;
OS Landranger 92

fence to the right until the
circular walk yellow arrows
indicate to follow the path
through a gate so a wall is
now on the left. The route
crosses the old railway
line and then continues,
providing lovely views of

Barnard Castle (if foliage
allows) and the surrounding
farmland.

▶ Enter the woods and
stay on the main path as
it cuts through the trees,
turning to the left and

Barnard Castle

dropping to join a track adjacent to Percy Beck. On reaching the beck, cut left along a track and then right over the bridge signed 'Town Centre' and climb the steps beyond to reach Raby Avenue, leading down to the town centre.

View to the meadow by River Tees

" A gentle, low-level walk with idyllic river scenery and a striking ruined abbey "

Barnard Castle is a fine old market town situated at the eastern end of Teesdale. Its main features are the splendid Bowes Museum and Art Gallery, the ruin of its 12th century castle at the western end of the town (see walk 17), and the ruined Egglestone Abbey to the east.

Ruins of Egglestone Abbey

Egglestone Abbey

North bank of River Tees opposite Eggleston Abbey

Route instructions

A Start this walk from the Galgate – the broad street in the centre of Barnard Castle. Walk down to the end of the street nearest the castle and then turn left, down the Horsemarket. Carry straight on beyond the Market Cross (which acts as a roundabout), down the Thorngate and across the footbridge beyond.

B Climb the slope on the far side of the river and turn left along a road. When the road ends carry on to join the tarmac road running through the caravan park ahead. Bear right along this, then cut left across a stile into a field, just before reaching the road. Walk along the left-hand edge of the field, and then continue across the three fields beyond to reach a tarmac road.

C Cut left along the road, passing the picturesque ruins of the 12th century Eggleston Abbey which are well worth a visit. Continue along the road for ¼ mile (0.5km) and then cut left, across the small road bridge over the river.

1 Eggleston Abbey ruins give a good impression of the abandoned Premonstratensian monastery founded in the late 12th century. The founders undertook preaching and pastoral work in the region and wore a white habit thus becoming known as the 'White Canons'.

Plan your walk

Berwick-upon-Tweed
Coldstream
Alnwick
Newcastle upon Tyne
Hexham
Sunderland
Durham
Barnard Castle
Middlesbrough
Darlington

DISTANCE: 3 miles (5km)

TIME: 1½ hours

START/END: NZ049166 Barnard Castle

TERRAIN: Easy

MAPS:
OS Explorer OL 31;
OS Landranger 92

walk 18 Egglestone Abbey **85**

D Once over the bridge cut left, off the road, onto a rough path which leads through dense woodland down to the riverside, where the trees give way on the right to open grazing land.

E Once the riverside path has passed the high fencing

around the sewage works, gradually curve right across a field towards a small stone ruin. On reaching this building cut right, up the hill towards a stile. Cross the stile and bear left to follow the path around a sports pitch with views of the grand Bowes Museum

Egglestone Abbey

building to the right. Go through the gate in the far corner of the field, turn right up a walled lane and then left at the road to return to the town centre or right to visit the Bowes Museum.

② The grand building of the Bowes Museum houses internationally significant collections of art. The structure was built in the 19th century by John and Joséphine Bowes who's passion for a wide range of arts led them to collect 15,000 objects from all over Europe between 1862 and 1874. Items varied from paintings and ceramics to textiles and furniture but sadly neither John or Joséphine lived to see the museum open in 1892 under the leadership of Trustees. The most famous object in the museum is a mechanical silver swan bought by the Bowes in 1872, which is over 200 years old and still in working order.

Bowes Museum from path

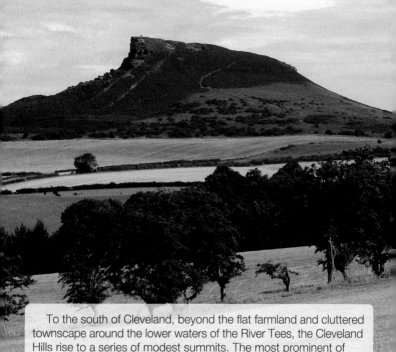

66 A short, steep climb to the summit of a landmark, rocky tor with superb panoramic views **99**

To the south of Cleveland, beyond the flat farmland and cluttered townscape around the lower waters of the River Tees, the Cleveland Hills rise to a series of modest summits. The most prominent of these, though not the highest, is the conical Roseberry Topping, with its distinctive rocky peak.

View of Roseberry Topping from the south

Roseberry Topping

View of Captain Cook's Monument
from Roseberry Topping

Route instructions

A From the car park at the southern end of Newton under Roseberry walk just beyond the northern end of the car park and turn right up a clear track between hedges, with fields beyond on either side. This track leads straight up to the edge of an oak wood which fringes the foot of the hill.

B Go through a gate into the wood. There are a number of paths through the trees ahead. For the easiest route turn hard left, then, after a short distance, double back to the right onto a good track which starts to climb the hill at a slant. The steep distinct stone path to the summit provides increasingly extensive views to the north and east.

1 Roseberry Topping was formed from sandstone laid down between 208 and 165 million years ago but its distinctive half-cone shape is a result of the hard sandstone cap protecting the lower layers of shales and clays from erosion. The previously conical summit changed shape in 1914 when a geological fault caused the summit to collapse though it is possible that the nearby mining of alum and ironstone was also a trigger. On a clear day the views extend to between 40 and 50 miles (60 to 80km) reaching as far as the Pennines. Closer features include the Cleveland Plain, the North Yorkshire Moors and the settlements along the Tees.

Plan your walk

DISTANCE: 2 miles (3km) with possible extensions

TIME: 1 hour

START/END: NZ570128 Newton under Roseberry

TERRAIN: Moderate; one climb of 750ft (230m)

MAPS:
OS Explorer OL 26;
OS Landranger 93

▶ From the peak there are many options. The map illustrates a possible loop to the north, but a number of other footpaths are clearly visible from the rocky summit, leading northeast to Guisborough and southwest to Great Ayton. In addition, the hill is crossed by the Cleveland Way, a long-distance footpath around the North York Moors. The Way passes Captain Cook's Monument (he was born at Marton, now on the southern outskirts of Middlesbrough) which is visible on a hill to the southeast.

Roseberry Topping

Northwest slope of Roseberry Topping

❝ Fine views, but not for the faint-hearted or for vertigo sufferers. A spectacular cliff-top walk, passing disused quarries along this dramatic coastline **❞**

Boulby is a tiny coastal village near the southern border of Cleveland, on the edge of the industrial area around the mouth of the River Tees. The area is dominated by the chimneys of the huge Boulby Potash Mine, the shafts and galleries of which reach out far under the North Sea. Site of the highest cliffs in England, these slopes were once mined for alum. These mines can still be seen from the cliff-top path.

Coastline near Sandsend, south of Boulby

Boulby

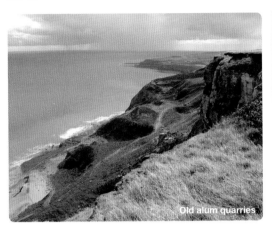

Old alum quarries

Route instructions

A Turn left in front of a row of cottages at the western edge of the village, which sit near the edge of the 350ft (100m) cliffs – the cliffs reach a height of 600ft (180m) further to the north. A path starts beyond the cottages, along the cliff edge. This path is a section of the Cleveland Way: a long-distance footpath 112 miles (180km) in length; leading north, from Filey in Yorkshire up the coast to Saltburn, then south, to Helmsley in the Yorkshire Moors.

B Follow the path along the cliffs until it cuts left, behind the bracken covered Rockhole Hill, before rejoining the cliffs beyond. North of Rockhole Hill, the cliffs are heavily indented

by the massive labours of the alum quarriers in past centuries.

C After a short distance, a footpath leads off to the left, past a triangulation pillar and on to the road. Cut left to complete the shortened version of this route. Otherwise, continue beside the quarries passing an information board explaining the manner and purpose of the alum industry.

1 This area is designated a Site of Special Scientific Interest due to its fossil content being significantly different from the surrounding area and the discovery of several pre-historic lizards both flying and marine.

Plan your walk

Berwick-upon-Tweed

Coldstream

Alnwick

Newcastle upon Tyne

Hexham

Sunderland

Durham

Barnard Castle

Middlesbrough

Darlington

DISTANCE: 2–4 miles (3–6.5km)

TIME: 1–2 hours

START/END: NZ760190 Boulby

TERRAIN: Moderate; climb of 350ft (110m)

MAPS: OS Explorer OL 27; OS Landranger 94

D Take the next footpath leading down to the left to Upton. Once the road is reached, turn left, back towards Boulby.

2 Boulby is an old Scandinavian place name meaning 'Bolli's Farm' and it appears in the Domesday Book of 1086 as 'Bolebi' or 'Bollebi'.

Boulby

View towards Teeside

Boulby Barns

Photo credits